More Experiments

Upon the Word

by
Susan Luke

Covenant Communications, Inc.

Copyright © 1998 by Susan Luke
All Rights Reserved
Printed in the United States of America
First Printing: August 1998

01 02 03 04   10 9 8 7 6 5 4 3

*More Experiments Upon the Word: Learning the
Gospel Through Fun & Easy Object Lessons*
Covenant Communications, Inc.
ISBN 1-57734-341-X
Cover Design by Val Bagley

To my family for their love, support, and patience!

TABLE OF CONTENTS

INTRODUCTION

I have been blessed with the wonderful opportunity of teaching seminary this past school year. I have learned, more so than ever, the value of a good object lesson. Christ, the greatest teacher of all, used everyday objects all the time when teaching gospel principles. A lesson that is seen, and not just heard, can have a lasting effect on those being taught. When an everyday object is used in teaching, the point of the lesson will be remembered every time the object is seen. I hope the students in my seminary class will always be reminded of the power of repentance when they see a moist towelette, or have the desire to anchor themselves to the scriptures when they use a vacuum cleaner (see pages 52 and 5). When you choose an experiment, practice it well until you are comfortable with your presentation. Preparation will help to make the experiment and application more memorable. I hope these ideas will be helpful in conveying gospel principles as you perform more experiments upon the word!

ADVERSITY BRINGS BLESSINGS

"For after much tribulation come the blessings."   D&C 58:4

•THINGS YOU WILL NEED
Backpack
Several heavy objects
Gift wrapping supplies

•EXPERIMENT
Wrap the various objects with gift wrap and label each gift with a different trial and possible blessing that could result from the trial. Place the wrapped objects in the backpack. Allow a class member to place the pack on their back to demonstrate its heaviness. At the appropriate time, take the gifts from the pack one at a time, discussing each trial and its corresponding blessing.

•GOSPEL APPLICATION
As you allow a class member to place the pack on their back, explain that trials and tribulations can sometimes be heavy burdens to carry. We can endure our trials more easily if we remember that often they bring blessings from Heavenly Father. D&C 58:4 states, "For after much tribulation come the blessings." After having the class member carry the heavy pack, remove the "trials" one at a time, discussing the blessing that each one brings.

1

Note: If desired, the gifts could contain treats or rewards that could be unwrapped and shared in class.

ANCHORED TO THE GOSPEL

"Lay hold upon the gospel of Christ, which shall be
set before you." Mormon 7:8

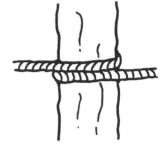

•THINGS YOU WILL NEED
Rope (approx. 20')
Access to a tree

•EXPERIMENT
Ask three people to hold one end of the rope, and
one person to hold the other end. At your signal,
have each side pull on the rope. It is easy for the
side with three to pull the rope from the one (or
at least pull it in their direction.) Now wrap the
rope once around the trunk of a tree. At your
signal, have each side pull again. The three
people can no longer pull the rope from the one.

•GOSPEL APPLICATION
The tree represents the gospel. When we anchor
ourselves to the gospel, things such as peace and
happiness cannot easily be pulled from us.

•ADDITIONAL APPLICATIONS

Commitment to the Lord—Without a true
commitment to serve the Lord, the adversary can
easily pull us around. But when we commit

3

ourselves to serving the Lord, we are given strength and support to resist the tuggings of the adversary and his followers.

Negative peer pressure—With the support of a loving family, church leaders, and a testimony of Jesus Christ, we can resist the pull of negative peer pressure.

ANCHORED TO THE SCRIPTURES

"Whoso [will] hearken unto the word of God, and [will] hold fast
unto it, they [will] never perish."   1 Nephi 15:24

•THINGS YOU WILL NEED
Vacuum cleaner
Scriptures
Paper people (see pattern on page 6)
Clear tape
Strips of paper labeled with worldly things, such
as unclean movies, immodest fashions, drugs and
alcohol, etc.

•EXPERIMENT
Cut out several paper people following the
pattern given on page 6. Fold back along the
dotted line so the paper people will stand freely.
Place several of the people on a table. Place the
rest of the people on top of the scriptures with
their feet taped securely to the scriptures. At the
appropriate time in the demonstration, vacuum
up the paper people. Those that are not anchored
to the scriptures will be "sucked into the world."

•GOSPEL APPLICATION
Nephi taught his brothers that "whoso would
hearken unto the word of God, and would hold
fast unto it, they would never perish;   neither

could the temptations and the fiery darts of the adversary overpower them unto blindness, to lead them away to destruction" (1 Nephi 15:24). The scriptures are the word of God. We can anchor ourselves firmly to the scriptures through diligent study of and obedience to the commandments contained therein. During the demonstration, discuss the prepared labels and tape them to the vacuum cleaner (the world). Turn on the vacuum. Run the hose over the people on the table to show how easy it is to be deceived and sucked into the world if not properly anchored. Now run the hose over the rest of the people. They are secure because they are anchored to the scriptures.

THE ATONEMENT

"There must be an atonement made, or else all mankind
must unavoidably perish." Alma 34:9

•THINGS YOU WILL NEED
Slightly scorched white cotton cloth
Clean white cotton cloth
Hydrogen peroxide (hair bleach)
Iron

•EXPERIMENT
Moisten the scorched cloth with the hydrogen
peroxide. Place the clean cloth over the
moistened cloth and iron until dry. The scorch
will be gone.

•GOSPEL APPLICATION
When a piece of clothing gets scorched, often it is
ruined and thrown out. Sin can ruin our lives
and cause us to be cast out eternally from
Heavenly Father's presence. Through the
Atonement, our lives can be cleansed, giving us
hope for a clean, bright eternal life.

•ADDITIONAL APPLICATIONS

Resurrection—We learn from Alma 11:43-45 that
through the resurrection "every thing shall be

restored to its perfect frame, as it is now, or in the body." Demonstrate this by removing the scorch from the cloth and restoring it to its "perfect frame."

AVOID EVIL INFLUENCES

"If sinners entice thee, consent thou not."   Proverbs 1:10

•THINGS YOU WILL NEED
Glass of water
One teaspoon of salt
Parchment paper
Rubber band
Dish containing water
Food coloring

•EXPERIMENT
Dissolve the teaspoon of salt in the glass of water and cover tightly with the parchment paper. Secure with the rubber band. Add several drops of food coloring to the water in the dish. Place the glass upside down in the dish. Eventually, the water in the glass will be colored also.

•GOSPEL APPLICATION
Often people think they are immune to the influence of evil, even when it is all around them.   Paul warns in Romans 16:17, "Now I beseech you, brethren, mark them which cause divisions and offences contrary to the doctrine which ye have learned; and avoid them."   1 Thessalonians 5:22 states, "Abstain from all appearance of evil." We cannot deceive ourselves

and think we are always strong enough to resist the many temptations the adversary throws at us. We cannot be surrounded by evil without it having some kind of effect on us. Demonstrate this by showing how the water in the glass is affected by the colored water in the dish—even though it is protected by the parchment paper.

BOUND BY SIN

"Lay aside every sin, which easily doth beset you, which
doth bind you down to destruction." Alma 7:15

•THINGS YOU WILL NEED
Large laundry bag with drawstring

•EXPERIMENT
Ask a class member to step inside the laundry bag.
As the presentation progresses, ask the class
member to "sink" into the laundry bag as you
drawstring it closed around their neck.

•GOSPEL APPLICATION
We can learn from the scriptures that sin binds us
down unto destruction (Alma 7:15). We also
learn that the devil leads us with a flaxen cord
until he can bind us with strong cords forever (2
Nephi 26:22). If we keep ourselves free from sin,
then we are able to perform the will of God more
easily. Demonstrate this by allowing the person to
step into the bag without pulling it up yet. The
person is still able to read scriptures, take the
sacrament, serve others, etc. But as sin sneaks in
and we are slowly led away with "flaxen cords," it
is much harder to perform the will of God.
Demonstrate this by pulling the laundry bag up to
the neck of the person and pulling snugly on the
drawstring. The person would now have a

11

difficult time reading scriptures, partaking of the sacrament, or serving others. We need to keep ourselves free from sin to avoid the binding power of the devil.

CHASTITY

"Keep thyself unspotted from the world."   D&C 59:9

•THINGS YOU WILL NEED

Clear drinking glass with water
Clay
Spoon

•EXPERIMENT

Place the glass of water on a table and tap it lightly
with the spoon. It should ring out with a clear
sound. During the presentation, place small
amounts of clay on the outside of the glass. Tap
lightly on the glass after each addition of clay. The
ringing sound becomes less and less clear until it
is just a "clank."

•GOSPEL APPLICATION

Paul counsels in 1 Timothy 4:12, "Let no man
despise thy youth; but be thou an example of the
believers, in word, in conversation, in charity, in
spirit, in faith, in purity." If we want to be an
example of purity, we need to "keep [ourselves]
unspotted from the world" (James 1:27). In the
demonstration, the clear glass of water represents
purity—ringing clear and true. When the clay,
which represents sin or transgression, is attached
to the glass, the sound is altered in a negative way.

13

Sin can alter our lives in a negative way also. By removing the clay from the glass, we can enjoy the beautiful sound once again. Through sincere repentance, we can once again enjoy a life of purity.

DEGREES OF GLORY

"There is one glory of the sun, and another glory of the moon, and another glory of the stars."   1 Corinthians 15:41

•THINGS YOU WILL NEED
Various ingredients (see experiment below)
Cracker
Biscuit
Cake with white frosting

•EXPERIMENT
Display the cracker, biscuit, and cake on a table. Display the various ingredients it would take to make each item.

•GOSPEL APPLICATION
Speaking of the Bible, Joseph Smith wrote, "It appeared self-evident from what truths were left, that if God rewarded every one according to the deeds done in the body, the term 'Heaven,' as intended for the Saints' eternal home, must include more kingdoms than one" (D&C 76, chapter heading).   Later he received a glorious vision of the three degrees of glory. Paul states in 1 Corinthians 15:41, "There is one glory of the sun, and another glory of the moon, and another glory of the stars: for one star differeth from another star in glory."   Compare this to the different "glory" of the baked items and their

15

corresponding ingredients. With only a few ingredients available, we can only hope to make a cracker. A few more ingredients will yield a biscuit or something similar. But with all the ingredients, we can make a grand and glorious cake with frosting (besides a multitude of other things.) Each kingdom allows us to accomplish certain things. The two lower kingdoms have their limits. We cannot hope to make a "grand and glorious cake" with what is available in those kingdoms. Only the celestial kingdom will stock the ingredients needed to accomplish such great things.

DISCERNMENT

"I will impart unto you of my Spirit which shall enlighten your
mind, which shall fill your soul with joy." D&C 11:13

•THINGS YOU WILL NEED
Scripture references written on strips of paper
A dark room

•EXPERIMENT
Prepare the room ahead of time by closing all
curtains and doing whatever else is needed in
order for the room to be completely dark when
the lights are turned off. Prepare and pass out to
class members the following scripture references:
D&C 88:67, Micah 7:8, 1 Peter 2:9, 1 John 1:5, Psalm
18:28. Before allowing class members to read their
scriptures, turn off the room lights—making it
difficult or impossible to read. At the appropriate
time, turn on the lights and have the class
members successfully read their scriptures.

•GOSPEL APPLICATION
The darkness of the room makes it difficult, if not
impossible, for the class members to read (or
discern) their scriptures. Just as the room lights
help the class members see what to read, the light
of the gospel helps us to see how to live our lives.

DISCOMFORT OF SIN

"Let your sins trouble you, with the trouble which shall
bring you down unto repentance."   Alma 42:29

•THINGS YOU WILL NEED
Small pebble or bean for each student

•EXPERIMENT
At the beginning of class, give each class member
a pebble or bean to place in their shoe. Have them
keep it there throughout the lesson.

•GOSPEL APPLICATION
Alma counseled his son, Corianton, to "let your
sins trouble you, with that trouble which shall
bring you down unto repentance" (Alma 42:29).
Just as the pebble causes physical discomfort, sin
causes spiritual discomfort through the
promptings of the Holy Ghost. To receive
physical relief, we can take the pebble out of the
shoe. Whereas, the only relief from sin is true
repentance.

DOUBT NOT

"And all things, whatsoever ye shall ask in prayer, believing, ye shall receive."   Matthew 21:22

•THINGS YOU WILL NEED
Large pitcher of water
Two clear bowls
Cup
Masking tape

•EXPERIMENT
Place a piece of tape near the top of one of the bowls. This will mark where the water level is to be. Ask one volunteer to come forward and slowly pour water into the bowl, up to the mark. Ask another volunteer to come forward and use the cup to scoop water out of the bowl as it is being filled. (The water from the cup can be emptied into the extra bowl.) Continue this process until all the water has been poured from the pitcher.

•GOSPEL APPLICATION
When teaching his disciples Jesus said, "For verily I say unto you, That whosoever shall say unto this mountain, Be thou removed, and be thou cast into the sea; and shall not doubt in his heart, but shall believe that those things which he saith shall come to pass; he shall have whatsoever he

19

saith. Therefore I say unto you, What things soever ye desire, when ye pray, believe that ye receive them, and ye shall have them" (Mark 11:23-24). In the demonstration, the water being poured into the bowl represents faith. The person is trying to fill the bowl to the mark. The water being taken from the bowl represents doubt. As long as we have doubt, we will never accomplish our desires. James 1:6 states, "But let him ask in faith, nothing wavering." The experiment could be performed again without doubt to show the successfulness of sufficient faith.

ENDURE TO THE END

"He that is faithful and endureth shall overcome
the world." D&C 63:47

•THINGS YOU WILL NEED

A sprouting potato
Pot filled with moist soil
Shoe box
Scrap cardboard
Tape

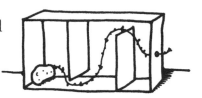

•EXPERIMENT

Plant the potato in the moist soil. Place the shoe
box on its side and place the pot in the corner of
the shoe box. Cut a hole in the shoe box at the
opposite end. Cut scraps of cardboard and tape in
place as shown in the diagram above to create a
maze. (Be sure to leave the appropriate gaps at
the top or bottom of the cardboard scraps so the
plant can grow through the maze.) Place the lid
securely on the shoe box and place it in a window.
After a few days, the shoot will have made its way
to the light.

•GOSPEL APPLICATION

We are promised eternal life if we "shall press
forward, feasting upon the words of Christ, and
endure to the end" (2 Nephi 31:20). Carefully

remove the lid from the shoe box and show how the sprout was determined to grow toward the light. By doing so, it was able to overcome the obstacles that were placed in its way. Through determination and commitment, we can overcome obstacles, endure to the end, and enjoy the blessings of eternal life.

• ADDITIONAL APPLICATIONS

Overcoming obstacles—We can more easily overcome any obstacle placed before us by focusing on the Light.

Diligence—"All victory and glory is brought to pass unto you through your diligence, faithfulnesss, and prayers of faith" (D&C 103:36).

More Experiments Upon the Word

ETERNAL BLISS

"Give heed to the word of Christ, which will point to you a
straight course to eternal bliss." Alma 37:44

•THINGS YOU WILL NEED
Two mirrors (one hand held, one larger)

•EXPERIMENT
Hold the hand mirror to your face (facing away
from you) as you stand in front of the larger
mirror. When adjusted correctly, you will see the
reflection continuing without end.

•GOSPEL APPLICATION
Alma counseled his son Helaman to "give heed
to the word of Christ, which will point to you a
straight course to eternal bliss" (Alma 37:44). To
get an idea of eternity, have the class members
take turns holding the hand mirror in front of the
larger mirror. If we follow the words of Christ, we
will enjoy eternal life.

FAITH

"If ye will have faith in me ye shall have power to do whatsoever thing is expedient in me." Moroni 7:33

•THINGS YOU WILL NEED
Clear goblet (or similar glass)
Dried peas
Dinner plate
Water

•EXPERIMENT
Fill the goblet to overflowing with peas. Carefully pour water up to the brim of the goblet and set it on the dinner plate. In a short while, the peas will swell and overflow onto the plate.

•GOSPEL APPLICATION
The dried peas in the goblet represent the many blessings that Heavenly Father has in store for us. We need to apply faith in order to "activate" the blessings. Moroni 10:7 states, "Wherefore I would exhort you that ye deny not the power of God; for he worketh by power, according to the faith of the children of men." Without faith on our part, Heavenly Father is limited in how much he can bless us. When we exercise faith, the blessings will swell and overflow in our lives.

•ADDITIONAL APPLICATIONS

Missionary Efforts—When we share the gospel with our nonmember friends and relatives, their hearts can begin to swell and overflow with the Spirit.

FELLOWSHIPPING

"He who loveth God loveth his brother also." 1 John 4:21

•THINGS YOU WILL NEED
Balloon
Measuring tape
Access to a refrigerator

•EXPERIMENT
Completely fill the ballon with air and tie it securely. Measure and note the circumference of the balloon. Place the ballon in a refrigerator for thirty minutes. Upon removal, measure and take note of the circumference again. The balloon should have shrunk in size.

•GOSPEL APPLICATION
Moroni taught that after someone is baptized and has received the Holy Ghost, they are then numbered among the people of the church, and their name is taken "that they might be remembered and nourished by the good word of God, to keep them in the right way, to keep them continually watchful unto prayer" (Moroni 6:4). As members of Christ's church, it is our duty to remember and nourish these new converts. If we fail to fellowship with sincere warmth and love, the testimony of the new members could become cold and shrink.

•ADDITIONAL APPLICATIONS

Spiritual warmth—Our spirits need continual warmth from the gospel. If they are left uncared for and spiritually cold, they will shrink.

THE HOLY GHOST

"Quench not the Spirit."   1 Thessalonians 5:19

•THINGS YOU WILL NEED
Small styrofoam container with lid
Alarm clock
Four washcloths

•EXPERIMENT
This presentation progresses in different steps. The first step is to sound the alarm clock. Next, sound the alarm and place it in the styrofoam container, then close the lid. The third step is to place four washcloths at the bottom of the container, sound the alarm and place it on top of the washclothes, then close the lid. With each step, the sound gets more muffled.

•GOSPEL APPLICATION
All of us who have repented, been baptized, and have received the gift of the Holy Ghost are entitled to his promptings. We can continue to enjoy the promtings of the Holy Ghost as long as we remain worthy. (This is represented by sounding the alarm.) John 8:47 states, "He that is of God heareth God's words: ye therefore hear them not, because ye are not of God." When we choose to sin, we are not of God and therefore

28

muffle the promptings of the Holy Ghost as demonstrated in the second and third steps of the presentation. The Lord warns in Mosiah 26:28, "Therefore I say unto you, that he that will not hear my voice, the same shall ye not receive into my church, for him I will not receive at the last day."

•ADDITIONAL APPLICATIONS

Muffled cries to the Lord—Speaking to the unrepentant, the Lord warns in Mosiah 11:24, "Yea, and it shall come to pass that when they shall cry unto me I will be slow to hear their cries; yea, and I will suffer them that they be smitten by their enemies." We also learn in John 9:31, "Now we know that God heareth not sinners: but if a man be a worshipper of God, and doeth his will, him he heareth." Do we muffle our cries to the Lord through unrepentant acts?

The needs of others—Do we hear the needs of others, or do we cover up their cries with other things in our lives? The washcloths and styrofoam container could represent various selfish desires that muffle the cries of others.

HUMILITY

"Be thou humble; and the Lord thy God shall lead thee by the hand,
and give thee answers to thy prayers." D&C 112:10

•THINGS YOU WILL NEED
Balloon
Wide-mouth jar

•EXPERIMENT
This experiment is done in two steps. The first
step is to blow air into the balloon, then while
holding tightly to the neck of the balloon, try to
use the filled balloon to lift the jar. The second
step is to let the air out of the balloon, then refill
the balloon while it is suspended in the mouth of
the jar. When the balloon is filled the second
time, it will press against the inside of the jar and
allow you to lift the jar as you lift the balloon.

•GOSPEL APPLICATION
James 4:10 states, "Humble yourselves in the sight
of the Lord, and he shall lift you up." In the
beginning of the experiment, the filled balloon
represents our being puffed up with pride. We are
not sufficiently humble to do as the Lord requests.
(This is represented by trying to lift the jar with
the filled balloon.) But when we strip ourselves
of pride and humble ourselves before the Lord
(deflate the balloon), we allow him to work

within us and lift us to the point where we can perform the labors that are requested by the Lord.

• ADDITIONAL APPLICATIONS

Strengthen thy brethren—In Luke 22:32, Christ said unto Simon, "When thou art converted, strengthen thy brethren." When we receive a testimony of the gospel of Jesus Christ, we need to use it to help strengthen and lift those around us.

Faith—D&C 8:10 reminds us that "without faith you can do nothing; therefore ask in faith." On the other hand, Mark 9:23 teaches us that "all things are possible to him that believeth." To demonstrate these principles, begin with an uninflated balloon. It is impossible to lift the jar with an uninflated balloon (representing a lack of faith). But when we are filled with faith, we have success. (Demonstrate this by filling the balloon with air while it is suspended inside the mouth of the jar.)

IN HIS IMAGE

"Let us make man in our image, after our likeness."   Genesis 1:26

•THINGS YOU WILL NEED
Picture from newspaper
Water
Turpentine
Liquid detergent
Spoon
Sponge
Plain paper
Small bowl

•EXPERIMENT
In a bowl, mix two spoonfuls of water, one spoonful of turpentine, and one spoonful of liquid detergent. Using the sponge, dab this mixture onto the newspaper picture. Lay a plain piece of paper over the top of the picture and rub vigorously with the back of a spoon. Carefully peel away the paper to reveal the image of the picture transferred to the plain paper.

•GOSPEL APPLICATION
God said in Genesis 1:26, "Let us make man in our image, after our likeness." Use the demonstration to show that an image is a direct resemblance of something else. By looking at our image, we can

32

determine God's image, just as the duplicate picture gives us an idea of what the original picture looks like.

•ADDITIONAL APPLICATIONS

Spreading the Gospel—We can spread the gospel with hard work and diligence (vigorously rubbing with the spoon.)

INVISIBLE SINS?

"Cleanse thou me from secret faults." Psalms 19:12

•THINGS YOU WILL NEED
Two clear glasses of water
Iodine
Clear lighter fluid

•EXPERIMENT
Display the clear glasses of water for the class to see. Place a few drops of iodine in one, and a few drops of lighter fluid in the other. (Note: If iodine and lighter fluid are not available, use red food coloring and water in separate containers labeled "Iodine" and "Lighter Fluid.")

•GOSPEL APPLICATION
Begin by explaining to the class that you have before them two different poisons—both equally dangerous. Place each poison in a glass and point out that it's easy to see the poison in the one glass and almost impossible to see the poison in the other. Explain that some transgressions are easy to see, like breaking the Word of Wisdom or swearing. Other sins like pride, lustful thoughts, and envy are harder to see, but are still just as serious. Are we sometimes guilty of judging others by their visible sins when we may have

34

"invisible" sins of our own? We need to be aware of these "invisible" sins and guard against them in our personal lives. (Note: If using actual poisons, be sure to use extra caution so that they are not ingested accidentally!)

LINKING GENERATIONS

"Whatsoever ye shall seal on earth shall be sealed in heaven."
Helaman 10:7

•THINGS YOU WILL NEED
Several 1" strips of paper
Stapler or tape
Ink pen
Scissors

•EXPERIMENT
On each strip of paper, write a member of a generation such as grandparents, parents, child, grandchild, etc. Make the strips into a paper chain by placing the "generations" in their proper order. Hold the chain for the class to see. At the appropriate time in the presentation, cut one of the links—allowing it, and the others attached to it, to fall to the floor.

•GOSPEL APPLICATION
In Helaman 10:7 the Lord said unto Nephi, "Behold, I give unto you power, that whatsoever ye shall seal on earth shall be sealed in heaven." Through this same sealing power, we have the opportunity to link many generations of family together. We have a responsibility to other generations to keep our link secure. If one link is broken, it can have devastating effects on all generations. At this point, cut whichever link

best fits your class. For example, if you are teaching several parents, cut the "parents" link to show how future generations can be cut off. Do we really want to be responsible for breaking the link in our families?

LOST SHEEP

"And if it so be that he find it, verily I say unto you, he rejoiceth more of that sheep, than of the ninety and nine which went not astray."
Matthew 18:13

•THINGS YOU WILL NEED
Old fluorescent light tube
Plastic wrap
Dark room

•EXPERIMENT
In a dark room, rub the fluorescent tube with plastic wrap. The tube will glow where it has been rubbed.

•GOSPEL APPLICATION
In Matthew 18:12-14, Jesus taught the parable of the lost sheep. This parable teaches us that all are important to the Lord, especially those who are lost. As members of Christ's church, it is our duty to find his lost sheep. We may find someone who appears to have lost all feeling toward the gospel, but with sincere love and fellowship, we can help them find the glow that is still within.

NOURISHED BY THE WORD OF GOD

"And their names were taken, that they might be remembered and
nourished by the good word of God." Moroni 6:4

•THINGS YOU WILL NEED
Two glasses of water
Salt
Spoon
Raisins or prunes

•EXPERIMENT
Stir as much salt as possible into **one** of the glasses
of water. Drop a few raisins or prunes into each
glass of water. Eventually the fruit in the plain
water will swell, while the fruit in the salt water
will not.

•GOSPEL APPLICATION
We can liken this experiment to the words found
in Alma 32:37-38. In these scriptures, the word of
the Lord is represented by a seed that has sprouted
into a tree. If we nourish the tree, it will take root,
grow up, and bring forth good fruit. If we fail to
nourish the tree, it will not take root and will
wither away. Alma adds in verse 39, "Now this is
not because the seed was not good, neither is it
because the fruit thereof would not be desirable;
but it is because your ground is barren, and ye will
not nourish the tree, therefore ye cannot have the

fruit thereof." Are we like the glass of salt water—not allowing the gospel to penetrate our lives and swell within us? Or, are we like the glass of plain water that nourishes the word of God and allows it to swell?

•ADDITIONAL APPLICATIONS

Bitterness of sin—The glass of salt water represents a life filled with sin. As long as sin (salt) is present, the person (fruit) goes unnourished spiritually. On the other hand, if a person's life is free from sin, it is much easier to be spiritually fed. This is demonstrated by the way the pure water penetrates and swells the fruit.

OBEDIENCE

"Blessed are they that hear the word of God, and keep it." Luke 11:28

•**THINGS YOU WILL NEED**
Recipe for cookies of your choice
Plate of cookies made from the recipe
One or two burned cookies

•**EXPERIMENT**
Display the plate of cookies, the recipe card, and the burned cookies.

•**GOSPEL APPLICATION**
Isaiah 1:19 states, "If ye be willing and obedient, ye shall eat the good of the land." In order to receive blessings from Heavenly Father, we must be obedient to his commandments. D&C 130:20-21 states, "There is a law, irrevocably decreed in heaven before the foundations of this world, upon which all blessings are predicated—And when we obtain any blessing from God, it is by obedience to that law upon which it is predicated." Demonstrate this fact by showing the plate of cookies. In order to have success in baking the cookies, the directions had to be followed carefully. If the proper baking time is ignored, the cookies could burn. What happens to people who do not follow the directions given

from the Lord? 3 Nephi 25:1 states, "For behold, the day cometh that shall burn as an oven; and all the proud, yea, and all that do wickedly, shall be stubble; and the day that cometh shall burn them up, saith the Lord of Hosts, that it shall leave them neither root nor branch."

OUR POTENTIAL

"Ye are gods; and all of you are children
of the most High." Psalms 82:6

•THINGS YOU WILL NEED
Balloon
Soft drink bottle

•EXPERIMENT
Place the uninflated balloon in the bottle with the open end of the balloon folded over the outside rim of the bottle's mouth. Hold the mouth of the bottle to your lips and try to blow up the balloon. It can't be done. By removing the restriction of the bottle, the ballon will blow up fine.

•GOSPEL APPLICATION
Sometimes through fear and self-doubt we limit ourselves—preventing us from reaching our potential. The Lord tells us in Psalms 82:6, "Ye are gods; and all of you are children of the most High." With this knowledge, we can remove the fears and doubts that hold us back, and we can then reach our true potential.

PARENTAL RESPONSIBILITIES

"Train up a child in the way he should go: and when he is old,
he will not depart from it."   Proverbs 22:6

•THINGS YOU WILL NEED
Strong magnet
Four paper clips

•EXPERIMENT
Suspend one paper clip from the magnet. Suspend the three paper clips magnetically from the first clip (do not actually hook the clips together).   When the first clip is removed from the magnet, most of the other clips fall.

•GOSPEL APPLICATION
As parents, we have a responsibility to teach our children the gospel through an example of righteous living.   D&C 68:25 states, "And again, inasmuch as parents have children in Zion, or in any of her stakes which are organized, that teach them not to understand the doctrine of repentance, faith in Christ the Son of the living God, and of baptism and the gift of the Holy Ghost by the laying on of the hands, when eight years old, the sin be upon the heads of the parents." Because of their unrighteous living, the Nephites were warned by Jacob, "Wherefore, ye shall

44

remember your children, how that ye have grieved their hearts because of the example that ye have set before them; and also, remember that ye may, because of your filthiness, bring your children unto destruction, and their sins be heaped upon your heads at the last day" (Jacob 3:10). The magnet represents the gospel. When we as parents are "staying connected" to the gospel through righteous living, our children have a better chance of staying connected. But if we fall away and remove ourselves from the gospel, our children risk falling also.

•ADDITIONAL APPLICATIONS

Blessings from the Lord—David said in Psalms 37:4, "Delight thyself also in the Lord; and he shall give thee the desires of thine heart." Moses said in Deuteronomy 28:2, "And all these blessings shall come on thee, and overtake thee, if thou shalt hearken unto the voice of the Lord thy God." The first paper clip represents us, the other clips represent the blessings given to us by hearkening unto the Lord. When we delight in the Lord and stay close to him (the magnet), then it is our privilege to have blessings "attached" to our lives. But when we remove ourselves from the Lord, our blessings fall away.

PRAY ALWAYS

"Men ought always to pray, and not to faint."   Luke 18:1

•THINGS YOU WILL NEED
Funnel with small opening
Clear glass bottle
Clay
Water
Straw

•EXPERIMENT
Place the funnel into the bottle and by using the clay, make an airtight seal around the mouth of the bottle. Pour water into the funnel. It should not flow into the bottle. At the appropriate time, place your finger over one end of the straw and push the other end through the funnel. Lift your finger. The water will now flow into the bottle.

•GOSPEL APPLICATION
D&C 19:38 states, "Pray always, and I will pour out my Spirit upon you, and great shall be your blessing." In order to receive blessings from Heavenly Father, we not only need to pray often, but with real intent. Mormon states in Moroni 7:9, "And likewise also is it counted evil unto man, if he shall pray and not with real intent of heart; yea, and it profiteth him nothing, for God

receiveth none such." Demonstrate the importance of prayer in obtaining blessings by stating
that the water represents blessings from Heavenly
Father. When the "blessings" are poured into the
funnel, they wait there until we do our part. The
straw represents sincere prayer. When we apply
"sincere prayer," the blessings are poured out
upon us.

•ADDITIONAL APPLICATIONS

Tithing—Malachi 3:10 states, "Bring ye all the
tithes into the storehouse, that there may be meat
in mine house, and prove me now herewith,
saith the Lord of hosts, if I will not open you the
windows of heaven, and pour you out a blessing,
that there shall not be room enough to receive it."
The water represents blessings from the Lord.
The straw represents tithing. When we pay our
tithing, we allow the Lord to pour out his
blessings upon us.

Faith and humility—D&C 105:12 states, "For
behold, I have prepared a great endowment and
blessing to be poured out upon them, inasmuch
as they are faithful and continue in humility
before me." The water represents blessings from
the Lord. The straw represents faith and humilty.
When we learn and apply these principles in our
lives, we are worthy to have great blessings
poured out upon us.

PRIORITIES

"To every thing there is a season, and a time to every purpose under the heaven."   Ecclesiastes 3:1

•THINGS YOU WILL NEED
Plastic spoon
Woolen cloth
Dish of puffed rice cereal

•EXPERIMENT
Charge the plastic spoon by rubbing it with the woolen cloth. Hold the spoon over the dish of puffed rice and watch as the cereal jumps to the spoon then shoots off in different directions.

•GOSPEL APPLICATION
"To every thing there is a season, and a time to every purpose under the heaven" (Eccl. 3:1). When we try to do everything at once, we usually end up making a big mess. We need to set our priorities.   We are taught in D&C 88:119, "Organize yourselves; prepare every needful thing; and establish a house, even a house of prayer, a house of fasting, a house of faith, a house of learning, a house of glory, a house of order, a house of God." If we learn to set our priorities, then we will have order and not confusion.

•ADDITIONAL APPLICATIONS

Envy and Strife—James 3:16 states, "For where envying and strife is, there is confusion and every evil work." Demonstrate this by rubbing the spoon on the woolen cloth to represent envy and strife. The results will be wild confusion as the puffed rice cereal shoots in every direstion. On the other hand, we learn in verses 17-18, "But the wisdom that is from above is first pure, then peaceable, gentle, and easy to be intreated, full of mercy and good fruits, without partiality, and without hypocrisy. And the fruit of righteousness is sown in peace of them that make peace." Hold a different spoon that has not been rubbed with the cloth over the rice. It should have a more "peaceable" result.

Gossip—The danger with gossiping is that once a story is told, you have no control of where it goes from there. Rub the spoon with the woolen cloth to represent the act of gossiping. Hold the spoon over the cereal and watch how the "story" flies out of control and in every direction.

PURIFICATION

"Wash thine heart from wickedness, that thou mayest be saved."
Jeremiah 4:14

•THINGS YOU WILL NEED
Clear glass jar with mud smeared on the inside
Bottle brush
Liquid dishwashing detergent
Dish towel
Tub or bowl with water

•EXPERIMENT
First try to clean the jar by wiping only the outside. Then place soap and water in the jar and use the bottle brush to clean the inside. Rinse, then dry with a towel.

•GOSPEL APPLICATION
In Moroni's epistle to Pahoran he states, "Now I would that ye should remember that God has said that the inward vessel shall be cleansed first, and then shall the outer vessel be cleansed also" (Alma 60:23). The commandment to purify our hearts is found many times throughout the scriptures. It's the first place we must cleanse if we are to become truly pure. To demonstrate the importance of cleansing the "inward vessel" first, try cleaning the jar by wiping the outside only. No matter how clean we get the outside, the

50

inside is still dirty and shows through. Now wash the inside with soap and water. When cleansed from the inside, the visible effect on the outside is automatically improved.

PURITY

"Lay hold upon every good gift, and touch not the evil gift, nor the unclean thing." Moroni 10:30

•THINGS YOU WILL NEED
Bowl of mud

•EXPERIMENT
Challenge a class member to place their bare hands in the mud without getting muddy. It can't be done successfully.

•GOSPEL APPLICATION
Mormon exhorted us in Moroni 10:30 to "touch not the evil gift, nor the unclean thing." Paul taught us to "cleanse ourselves from all filthiness of the flesh and spirit" (2 Corinthians 7:1). Our world is full of movies, television shows, music, and activities that are covered with spiritual mud and filthiness. No matter what others say, participating in these things will affect us spiritually. As demonstrated, we just can't play in the mud without getting muddy!

•ADDITIONAL APPLICATIONS

Repentance—Along with the bowl of mud, you will also need moist towelettes and a white dress or shirt for this experiment. The mud represents sin and the white clothing represents the kingdom of heaven. The moist towelettes represent repentance. Begin by placing your hands in the bowl of mud, then act like you're going to put on the white piece of clothing. Ask if it would be possible for you to put on the clothing without getting it dirty. Of course not. Ask someone to read 3 Nephi 27:19. It is impossible for any unclean thing to enter the kingdom of heaven. Ask someone to continue by reading verse 20. In order to stand spotless before God, we must repent. Demonstrate this by washing your hands with the moist towelettes. It may take some work to get your hands clean, just as it takes work to complete the process of repentance. If you cleanse yourself from all sin and endure to the end, you will be saved in the kingdom of heaven. Demonstrate this by putting on the white clothing with your clean hands.

RECORD KEEPING

"Write the things which you have seen and heard."   3 Nephi 27:23

•THINGS YOU WILL NEED
Paper and pencil for each class member

•EXPERIMENT
Pass out the paper and pencils and challenge each class member to write down the events of any ordinary day that happened a year ago, six months ago, one month ago, a week ago.

•GOSPEL APPLICATION
When Christ visited the people of ancient America, he said unto Nephi, "Bring forth the record which ye have kept" (3 Nephi 23:7). Nephi did as the Lord requested. When Christ looked over the records, he saw that they were not complete—some important events were left out. What would we do if Christ appeared to us and asked for our personal or family record? Would the records be complete? We can follow Nephi's example of obedience by completing the records in our charge (verse 13).

RESURRECTION

"They can die no more; their spirits uniting with their
bodies, never to be divided." Alma 11:45

•THINGS YOU WILL NEED
Clear glass jar with tight-fitting lid
Clear container of water
Clear container of oil
Egg

•EXPERIMENT
Display the water, oil, and egg on a table. At the
appropriate time in the presentation, place equal
parts of water and oil in the jar, leaving a small
amount of room at the top of the jar. Fasten the
lid tightly. During the presentation, shake the jar
then allow it to sit. Add the egg, shake, and allow
it to sit again.

•GOSPEL APPLICATION
At the beginning of our earthly life, our spirit
enters our body and continues to dwell there until
death. Demonstrate this by adding the oil (the
spirit) to the water (the body) and shaking (life).
At death, our spirit separates from the body. This
is represented by letting the mixture sit until
separated. Our spirit and body remain in this state
of separation until the resurrection. Speaking of
the resurrection, Alma said, "I say unto you that

this mortal body is raised to an immortal body, that is from death, even from the first death unto life, that they can die no more; their spirits uniting with their bodies, never to be divided; thus the whole becoming spiritual and immortal, that they can no more see corruption" (Alma 11:45). Demonstrate this by adding the egg (representing new life) to the oil and water. Shake and let sit. This time the oil (the spirit) and the water (the body) no longer separate. (Note: There may be some foam that accumalates at the top after shaking, but the oil and water won't separate. To get rid of the foam, pour the mixture gently back and forth between two containers.)

SATAN'S INFLUENCE

"And he became Satan, yea, even the devil, the father of all lies,
to deceive and to blind men."   Moses 4:4

•THINGS YOU WILL NEED
Two plastic bags
Narrow wooden stick (approx. 18" long)
Thumb tack with flat head
Vinegar
Baking soda
Glass

•EXPERIMENT
Place the plastic bags at each end of the stick as
shown on page 58.   Place the thumbtack at the
corner of a table with the point facing up.
Carefully balance the stick on the tack.   Pour some
soda and vinegar into a glass.   As it begins to fizz,
carefully tilt the glass over one of the bags.   The
gas produced is heavier than air and should make
the balance uneven.

•GOSPEL APPLICATION
The New Testament speaks of Jesus healing those
"that were oppressed of the devil" (Acts 10:38).
We may not be able to see the devil or his
followers, but their influence can weigh heavily
upon us.   Demonstrate this by showing how the
invisible gas in the plastic bag weighs it down and

makes the balance uneven. We must always guard against Satan's "invisible" tactics.

•ADDITIONAL APPLICATIONS

Humility—Alma taught the poor among the Zoramites that since their afflictions compelled them to be humble, they would be blessed. But he went on to teach that greater blessings would come to those who truly humbled themselves without being compelled to be humble (Alma 32:12-16). James 4:10 states, "Humble yourselves in the sight of the Lord, and he shall lift you up." True humility (the invisible gas) is necessary to be lifted up and exalted.

SHARING TALENTS

"To every man is given a gift by the Spirit of God...that all
may be profited thereby."   D&C 46:11-12

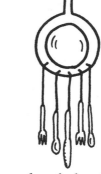

•THINGS YOU WILL NEED
Frying pan
Six eating utensils
Tape
String

•EXPERIMENT
Tie a 12"-18" piece of string to each of the five
utensils (one utensil is set aside).   At the
appropriate time in the presentation, tape the end
of each string inside the frying pan as shown
above. Strike the utensils with the extra utensil to
produce a pleasing sound.

•GOSPEL APPLICATION
D&C 46:11-12 states, "For all have not every gift
given unto them; for there are many gifts, and to
every man is given a gift by the Spirit of God. To
some is given one, and to some is given another,
that all may be profited thereby." To demonstrate
this principle, hand out the utensils to various
class members stating a talent that each possesses.
Their individual talents may be exceptional, but
unless shared, they profit no one. When brought
together, talents can be magnified and enjoyed by

all. Ask the class members to come forward with their "talents" and tape them to the inside bottom of the frying pan. Hold the frying pan in the air and make a lovely sound by striking the utensils.

•ADDITIONAL APPLICATIONS

Faith without works—We may have faith that the utensils can make a beautiful sound when united together, but if we don't apply the "works" by attaching them to the frying pan, our faith will be in vain. James 2:17 states, "Even so faith, if it hath not works, is dead, being alone." We continue to learn in verse 24, "Ye see then how that by works a man is justified, and not by faith only."

SHATTERED IMAGE

"A talebearer revealeth secrets: but he that is of a faithful
spirit concealeth the matter."   Proverbs 11:13

•THINGS YOU WILL NEED
Two inexpensive hand mirrors (framed with
metal or plastic)
Heavy paper sack
Hammer
Glass cleaner
Soft cloth

•EXPERIMENT
Place one of the mirrors in the paper sack and
close it tightly. At the appropriate time, carefully
crack the mirror (while in the sack) with the
hammer. Later in the demonstration, clean and
shine the other mirror with glass cleaner.

•GOSPEL APPLICATION
Ask a class member to come forward and look in
the mirror. Comment on the perfect image that
reflects from the mirror. Now place the mirror in
the paper sack and carefully hit it with the
hammer. Pull the mirror from the sack and have
the class member look again at their reflection.
This time the image is imperfect. No matter how
hard we try, the image cannot be restored to its

original state. This is similar to the effects of gossip. When we speak evil of others, we shatter their image—making restoration impossible. Paul taught the Ephesians, "Let no corrupt communication proceed out of your mouth, but that which is good to the use of edifying, that it may minister grace unto the hearers." This advice is still true today. Instead of shattering someone's image by gossiping, we can help to polish their image by using words that edify and uplift them. Demonstrate this by polishing the other mirror using the glass cleaner and soft cloth. Ask the class member to look into the polished mirror—commenting on the perfect image that is reflected.

•ADDITIONAL APPLICATIONS

The final judgment—When speaking of the final judgment Alma said, "And it is requisite with the justice of God that men should be judged according to their works; and if their works were good in this life, and the desires of their hearts were good, that they should also, at the last day, be restored unto that which is good" (Alma 41:3). On the other hand, "If their works are evil they shall be restored unto them for evil" (Alma 41:4). Will our works on this earth cause our eternal reflection to be cracked and distorted, or beautifully polished? Have class members take turns viewing themselves in each mirror.

SINS REVEALED

"But behold, ye cannot hide your crimes from God." Alma 39:8

•THINGS YOU WILL NEED
White paper
Milk
Small paintbrush
Iron

•EXPERIMENT
Using the small paintbrush and milk, write various sins on the white paper. As the milk dries, the writing should become almost invisible. During the presentation, heat the iron and run it over the paper. The writing should now appear.

•GOSPEL APPLICATION
Many people are under the false impression that they can hide their sins from the Lord. The Lord says in Jeremiah 16:17, "For mine eyes are upon all their ways: they are not hid from my face, neither is their iniquity hid from mine eyes." Alma 39:8 states, "But behold, ye cannot hide your crimes from God; and except ye repent they will stand as a testimony against you at the last day." We may be able to hide our sins from others, but God knows our sins and they are recorded. When the Lord comes again, he will "bring to light the

hidden things of darkness, and will make manifest the counsels of the hearts" (1 Corinthians 4:5). Demonstrate this by running the iron over the paper to reveal the hidden sins.

•ADDITIONAL APPLICATIONS

Service to others—In the Sermon on the Mount, Jesus taught that we should do our service to others in secret. By so doing, Heavenly Father will reward us openly (see Matthew 6:1-4). Use the paintbrush and milk to write various acts of service on the white paper. When dry, use the iron to reveal these secret acts.

Pray in secret—In the Sermon on the Mount, Jesus taught that we should pray in secret. When we do so, Heavenly Father rewards us openly (Matthew 6:5-6). Use the paintbrush and milk to write Matthew 6:6 (or at least part of it) on the white paper. When dry, use the iron to represent how our secret prayers are known to God.

SMALL ACTS OF SERVICE

"And out of small things proceedeth that which is great." D&C 64:33

•THINGS YOU WILL NEED
Five or six marbles
Flat ruler with groove down the center

•EXPERIMENT
Place the ruler flat on the table. Place all but one of the marbles on the groove of the ruler touching each other. Roll the extra marble against the line of marbles on the ruler. The marble at the opposite end will roll away.

•GOSPEL APPLICATION
D&C 64:33 states, "Be not weary in well-doing, for ye are laying the foundation of a great work. And out of small things proceedeth that which is great." Sometimes we may feel like our small acts of service are not helping, but according to the demonstration, we never know the effect they have on the other end.

•ADDITIONAL APPLICATIONS

Gossip—The spreading of stories at one end can affect someone at the other end—usually in an adverse way.

Good works—Galations 6:7 states, "For whatsoever a man soweth, that shall he also reap." If we sow good works all our days, then we shall reap the same. The demonstration shows that one marble "reaps" one marble at the other end. Two marbles rolled into the line of marbles "reaps" two marbles at the other end. Three "reaps" three, and so on.

SOFTENED BY AFFLICTIONS

"Many were softened because of their afflictions, insomuch that
they did humble themselves before God." Alma 62:41

•THINGS YOU WILL NEED
Two hard-boiled eggs
One cup of vinegar

•EXPERIMENT
Place one of the hard-boiled eggs into the cup of
vinegar and allow it to sit for one week. This will
allow the shell to become softened. Prior to the
presentation, remove the egg, rinse, and pat dry.
Allow both eggs (still in their shells) to be passed
around the class during the presentation.

•GOSPEL APPLICATION
We read in Alma 62:41, "But behold, because of
the exceedingly great length of the war between
the Nephites and the Lamanites many had
become hardened, because of the exceedingly great
length of the war; and many were softened
because of their afflictions, insomuch that they
did humble themselves before God, even in the
depth of humility." When faced with afflictions,
do we blame God for our troubles—allowing
ourselves to become hardened like the regular
hard-boiled egg? Or, do we allow the afflictions to
soften and humble us like the vinegar-soaked
egg?

SPIRITUAL DIFFERENCES

"For man looketh on the outward appearance, but
the Lord looketh on the heart."   1 Samuel 16:7

•**THINGS YOU WILL NEED**
Pineapple
Coconut
Apple
Other fruit, if desired
Basket (optional)

•**EXPERIMENT**
Display the basket of fruit on the table in view of
the class. During the presentation, each fruit will
be compared to the others.

•**GOSPEL APPLICATION**
Point out to the class that each piece of fruit is
similar in that they are all fruit, but each has
different qualities and different exteriors. We too
are all similar to each other in that we are all
children of God, but we have different qualities,
exteriors, and levels of spirituality. We each have
a precious spirit inside; some are buried deep
within and harder to get to, while some spirits are
close to the surface.   Demonstrate this by
comparing the different surfaces of the fruit. It is
easy to enjoy the tender fruit of the apple, because
its skin is quite thin. A pineapple is a different

story, however. Its skin is rough and prickly, making it more difficult to enjoy the sweet fruit within. A coconut is nearly impossible to open. Extra tools are needed to enjoy its contents. When we view others, we need to remember that everyone has something wonderful inside, even if the exterior is a little hard to get through.

STRENGTH IN UNITY

"Be perfectly joined together in the same mind and
in the same judgment." 1 Corinthians 1:10

•THINGS YOU WILL NEED
Two yardsticks
Tape measure
Two clamps
Two chairs
String with heavy weight attached

•EXPERIMENT
Place the two chairs back to back, about 2 1/2' apart.
Place the yardsticks across the backs of the chairs,
one stick on top of the other. Tie the weight to the
center of the sticks and allow it to hang down
without touching the ground. Measure the
distance between the low point of the sticks and
the floor to see how much bending has taken
place. Next, clamp the sticks together at each end
and replace them on the backs of the chairs.
Allow the weight to hang down once more and
measure the distance again. The sticks will bend
less this time, because they are unified and
strengthened by the clamps.

•GOSPEL APPLICATION
Paul taught the Corinthians to "be perfectly joined
together in the same mind and in the same

judgment" (1 Corinthians 1:10). When, as a group, we have a task to complete, we will find more strength to finish the project when we are unified in mind and purpose. This is demonstrated by the decrease of bending the yardsticks show when clamped together in unity.

•ADDITIONAL APPLICATIONS

A second witness—On its own (start with only one yardstick), the Bible is subject to many interpretations by many people. The principles can be "bent" according to the one interpreting. When you add the Book of Mormon (apply and clamp the second yardstick), you give strength to the principles taught in the Bible, and less bending occurs. The Lord says in Ezekial 37:16-17, "Moreover, thou son of man, take thee one stick, and write upon it, For Judah, and for the children of Israel his companions: then take another stick, and write upon it, For Joseph, the stick of Ephraim, and for all the house of Israel his companions: And join them one to another into one stick; and they shall become one in thine hand."

STRENGTH THROUGH PRAYER

"And it shall come to pass, that whosoever shall call on the
name of the Lord shall be delivered." Joel 2:32

•THINGS YOU WILL NEED
Three tumblers
A sheet of writing paper

•EXPERIMENT
Lay the sheet of paper like a bridge across two of
the tumblers. Place the third tumbler on the
"bridge." The bridge collapses and the tumbler
falls. At the appropriate time in the presentation,
fold the paper accordian-style lengthwise. Again,
place it across the tumblers and replace the third
tumbler. This time, the reinforced paper will
support the weight of the tumbler.

•GOSPEL APPLICATION
While being persecuted by Amulon, the people of
Alma prayed mightily to God for support. When
Amulon commanded them to stop their cries to
God, they continued to "pour out their hearts to
him" (Mosiah 24:12). Because of their
willingness to submit to the Lord, they were
strengthened and were able to bear their burdens
with ease (Mosiah 24:15). When we feel the
pressure of burdens upon our back (the tumbler),

we need to follow the prayerful example of Alma and his people. The Lord will strengthen us also (paper folding) if we are willing to "submit cheerfully and with patience" (Mosiah 24:15) to him.

•ADDITIONAL APPLICATIONS

Strengthen others—Luke 22:32 states, "and when thou art converted, strengthen thy brethren." This can happen in more ways than one. If we learn a point of doctrine that helps our testimony to grow, then we should share it with other Church members to strenghthen and uplift them. If we have new converts in our ward, then we should strengthen them with continual love and support until they are deeply rooted in the gospel. In both cases, the other Church member and the new convert are represented by the unfolded piece of paper. Discuss ways to strengthen others in both situations as you fold the piece of paper.

THOUGHTS

"For as he thinketh in his heart, so is he." Proverbs 23:7

•THINGS YOU WILL NEED
String with large nail tied to one end
(could be any small weighted object)

•EXPERIMENT
Hold the string with the weight suspended below. Without moving your hand, think strongly about the weight moving in a circle. It will probably do so without visible movement of the hand. You can also think of it moving back and forth or side to side.

•GOSPEL APPLICATION
Thoughts control our actions. Proverbs 23:7 states, "For as he thinketh in his heart, so is he." Before our actions are played out, they must begin as a thought in our mind. Show the power of thought by presenting the experiment. Speaking of the consequences of uncontrolled thoughts, King Benjamin makes it clear when he states, "But this much I can tell you, that if ye do not watch yourselves, and your thoughts, and your words, and your deeds, and observe the commandments of God, and continue in the faith of what ye have heard concerning the coming of our Lord, even unto the end of your lives, ye

must perish. And now, O man, remember, and perish not." Although we place a good deal of emphasis on controlling bad thoughts, equal emphasis should be focused on the power of good thoughts. In order to reach our righteous goals, we must first see them in our mind.

TITHING

"And of all that thou shalt give me I will surely
give the tenth unto thee."   Genesis 28:22

•THINGS YOU WILL NEED

One clear 9 x 13 baking dish (or similar)
Two clear pint-size jars
Large container of water with large opening
Medium container of water with medium
opening
Eyedropper of water

•EXPERIMENT

Label one of the jars "MYSELF" and one of the
jars "THE LORD." Place the two pint jars in the
baking dish and display on a table. At the
appropriate times in the presentation, pour water
from the containers into the jars.

•GOSPEL APPLICATION

Malachi 3:10 states, "Bring ye all the tithes into the
storehouse, that there may be meat in mine
house, and prove me now herewith, saith the
Lord of hosts, if I will not open you the windows
of heaven, and pour you out a blessing, that there
shall not be room enough to receive it." What is
our personal commitment to the law of tithing?
Do we give it in small amounts—and grudgingly?
Are we careful to give only what is required and

nothing more? Or, do we give fully and willingly? Demonstrate these various attitudes toward tithing by using the eyedropper to represent one who gives grudgingly, the jar with a medium-sized opening to represent someone who gives just enough, and the jar with a large-sized opening who gives freely and willingly. With each container, pour some of the "tithing" into the Lord's jar. Now discuss with the class what kind of blessings they would like to receive from the Lord. Do they want an eyedropperful of blessings? A medium amount of blessings? Or, do they want the blessings to overflow in their lives—so much that there will not be room enough to receive it? With each corresponding container, pour some of the blessings into the jar labeled "MYSELF." Finish by filling the jar to overflowing with the large container.

•ADDITIONAL APPLICATIONS

Generosity—Deuteronomy 15:11 states, "Thou shalt open thine hand wide unto thy brother, to thy poor, and to thy needy, in thy land." For this demonstration you will need only one of the pint jars labled "THE NEEDY." Challenge the class to think about their attitude toward helping others. Are they represented by the eyedropper—one who complains and gives only a little? Are they represented by the jar with the medium-sized opening—giving only what they have to? Or, are they like the large jar—giving cheerfully and completely?

TRIAL OF YOUR FAITH

"Ye receive no witness until after the trial of your faith."   Ether 12:6

•THINGS YOU WILL NEED
Raw milk (or heavy cream)
Small glass jar with tight-fitting lid
Salt (optional)
Bread or rolls (optional)

•EXPERIMENT
Allow the milk or cream to sit in a warm place for 24-36 hours. Place in a sealed jar and shake vigorously until chunks of butter form. Pour off excess liquid and rinse with water. Add salt as needed. Spread butter on bread or roll and enjoy.

•GOSPEL APPLICATION
Ether 12:6 teaches us that "ye receive no witness until after the trial of your faith." When faced with a trial, often we will not see the blessing until after the trial has passed. When we have completed the trial by exercising faith in Jesus Christ, then we can enjoy the resulting blessings. Demonstrate this by following the directions to make butter. Enjoy the "blessings" from the "trial" by spreading the butter on a piece of bread and partaking of it.

TWO OR THREE WITNESSES

"In the mouth of two or three witnesses every
word may be established."   Matthew 18:16

•THINGS YOU WILL NEED
Large button
Two kitchen forks
Cup

•EXPERIMENT
When you place the edge of the button on the rim
of the cup, it will fall off at once. When you place
the forks on the button as shown in the diagram
above, the button will balance on the rim.

•GOSPEL APPLICATION
In a court of law, witnesses help prove the
truthfulness of a story. It's hard to accept a story as
truth if it can only be verified by one person. In
Matthew 18:16 the Lord says, "That in the mouth
of two or three witnesses every word may be
established."   The Lord followed through with
these words when he brought forth the Book of
Mormon as another testament of Jesus Christ.
The Lord called for witnesses to testify of seeing
the gold plates that Joseph Smith translated. On
its own, a story may not be credible. With
witnesses, it will be supported and established.
Demonstrate this by showing how the button falls

by itself, but is supported with the help of the forks.

• ADDITIONAL APPLICATIONS

Service to others—The button in the demonstration represents someone in need of help. Without support, they continue to fall. We may be afraid to help, in fear that we may fall also. D&C 6:33 states, "Fear not to do good, my sons, for whatsoever ye sow, that shall ye reap; therefore, if ye sow good ye shall also reap good for your reward." We will receive blessings when we exercise courage and a willingness to help others. Demonstrate this by showing how the button can balance successfully with the help of the forks.

UNITED IN ALL THINGS

"Be determined in one mind and in one heart,
united in all things." 2 Nephi 1:21

•THINGS YOU WILL NEED
Two or more walnuts in shells

•EXPERIMENT
It is difficult or impossible to crack a walnut by squeezing it in your hand. However, by squeezing two walnuts together in the hand, one cracks easily.

•GOSPEL APPLICATION
2 Nephi 1:21 states, "Be determined in one mind, and in one heart, united in all things." Sometimes when we're working alone, it's hard to get a job done. In Ecclesiastes 4:9 we learn, "Two are better than one; because they have a good reward for their labour." When we unite with others to accomplish a common goal, we tend to have greater success.

•ADDITIONAL APPLICATIONS

Book of Mormon—Using the Bible alone, it is hard to "crack" some of the mysteries of God. With the help of the Book of Mormon, we can break down some of these mysteries and have a better understanding of gospel principles.

Fellowshipping—Before we can "crack" the shell of someone we are trying to teach or fellowship, we need to find common ground, hobbies, or interests with the person. When we do this, we build relationships of trust and are then able to "crack" the barriers that surround them.

UNKIND WORDS

"Keep thy tongue from evil, and thy lips from
speaking guile."   Psalm 34:3

•THINGS YOU WILL NEED
Empty bottle
Small slip of paper
Pencil

•EXPERIMENT
At the appropriate time, write upon the slip of
paper a few unkind words and roll the paper into
a ball. Hold the bottle horizontally and place the
paper ball just inside the neck. Try to blow the
ball into the bottle. Instead of going into the
bottle, it will fly back toward your face.

•GOSPEL APPLICATION
We are advised to "keep thy tongue from evil,
and thy lips from speaking guile" (Psalm 34:13).
This advice not only protects others, but protects
ourselves. When we use unkind words, often
they return to us in undesirable ways. Demonstrate this by writing the unkind words on the slip
of paper and performing the experiment as
directed. Another good piece of advice can be
found in Proverbs 21:23: "Whoso keepeth his
mouth and his tongue keepeth his soul from
troubles."

INDEX

Light, of Christ, 17, 21
Listening, to the needs of others, 29
    to the Holy Ghost, 28
Lost sheep, 38

Missionary, efforts, 25, 33

Nourished, by the word of God, 26, 39

Obedience, 41
Obstacles, overcoming, 22
Organize, yourselves, 48

Parents, responsibility to children, 36, 44
Peer pressure, negative, 4
Potential, 43
Prayer, 46
    muffled, 29
    secret, 64
    strength through, 72
Priorities, 48
Purification, 50
Purity, 52, 13

Record keeping, 54
Repentance, 18, 52
Revealed, sins, 63
Responsibilities, parental, 36, 44
Resurrection, 7, 55

OTHER BOOKS BY SUSAN LUKE

SUPER SUNDAYS!
Games, puzzles, service projects, music, and more are included in this treasure trove of Sabbath activities. From creating an Articles of Faith mobile, to performing a puppet show using scripture characters, to playing Book of Mormon Dominoes or Gospel Bingo, these activities are fun, interesting, varied, simple to do, and help teach important gospel principles. Best of all, they can be done reverently in keeping with the spirit of the Sabbath.

LITTLE TALKS FOR LITTLE PEOPLE
Includes text and visual aids for a dozen brief talks that children can learn quickly and enjoy presenting. Subjects like: "Love Everyone," "A Happy Home," "Noah and His Ark," "Wiggles," "Let Your Light Shine," and seven more. Short sentences make them excellent for very young children. Simple, thorough instructions show a child exactly how to prepare the visual aids and give presentations.

MORE LITTLE TALKS FOR LITTLE PEOPLE
This volume provides text and visual aids for a baker's dozen brief talks that children can learn quickly and enjoy presenting. Subjects include "My Testimony," "Daniel and the Lion's Den," "Prayer," "Songs of the Heart," "Tithing," "The True Meaning of Christmas," and seven more. These talks are so simple that an older child can easily

help a younger brother or sister to prepare and present them. Both the "big people" and "little people" in your family will enjoy them for years to come!

FANTASTIC FAMILY NIGHTS!

Here's a book that has everything you need to quickly plan effective, fun, creative family nights. This book includes ideas for games, activities, lessons, charts, and visual aids. You will find a wealth of resources that will help you fulfil your responsibility to your family without having to spend undue amounts of time in preparation.

AWESOME FAMILY NIGHTS

Here's help to make family home evening the week's biggest attraction! Thirteen lessons teach children important gospel principles in fun, interesting ways; and the book includes excellent ideas for a variety of games, activities, charts, visual aids, and even refreshments.

POSITIVELY PRIMARY

If you're a Primary leader or teacher, you need this book! In these pages you'll find a wealth of simple, clever, workable ideas that you can use to make your Primary meetings more colorful, efficient, fun, and inviting. From ribbons and certificates for special recognition, to lively classroom and seating markers, to "Wow! What a Class" posters, to Primary newsletters, journals, and "Clutter Control" badges, you'll have the tools you need to make even the most ordinary Primary something extraordinary!